Being Like Butterflies

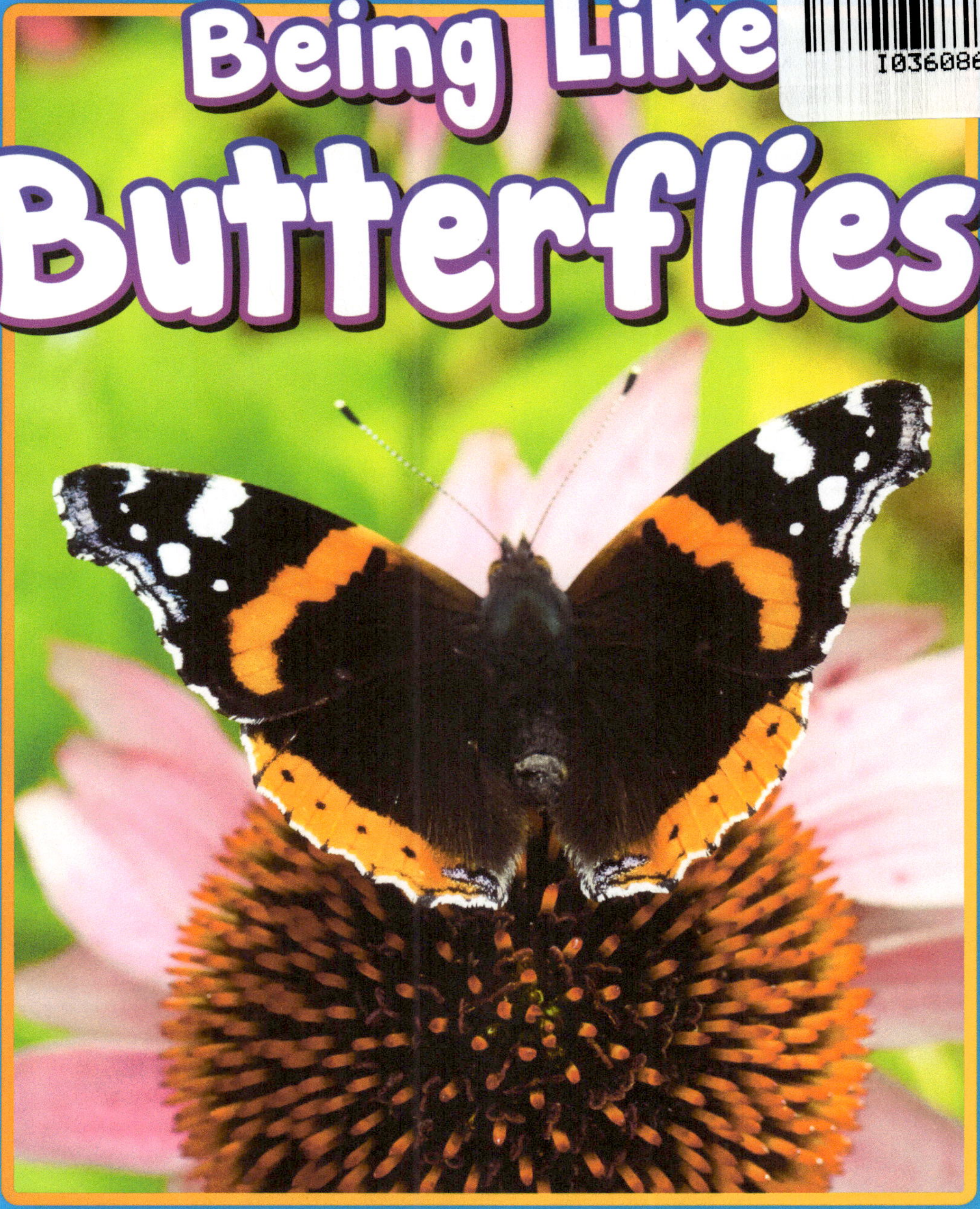

Dona Herweck Rice

Smithsonian

© 2019 Smithsonian Institution. The name "Smithsonian" and the Smithsonian logo are registered trademarks owned by the Smithsonian Institution.

Consultants

Brian Mandell
Program Specialist
Smithsonian Science Education Center

Chrissy Johnson, M.Ed.
Teacher, Cedar Point Elementary
Prince William County Schools, Virginia

Sara Cooper, M.Ed.
Third Grade Teacher
Fullerton School District

Publishing Credits

Rachelle Cracchiolo, M.S.Ed., *Publisher*
Conni Medina, M.A.Ed., *Editor in Chief*
Diana Kenney, M.A.Ed., NBCT, *Series Developer*
Emily R. Smith, M.A.Ed., *Content Director*
Véronique Bos, *Creative Director*
Robin Erickson, *Art Director*
Michelle Jovin, M.A., *Associate Editor*
Mindy Duits, *Series Designer*
Kevin Panter, *Senior Graphic Designer*
Smithsonian Science Education Center

Image Credits: p.7 Kjell B. Sandved/Science Source; p.14 Mark Bowler/Science Source; p.14 Phil Degginger/Science Source; all other images from iStock and/or Shutterstock.

Library of Congress Cataloging-in-Publication Data

Names: Rice, Dona, author. | Smithsonian Institution, author.
Title: Being like butterflies / Dona Herweck Rice, Smithsonian.
Description: Huntington Beach, CA : Teacher Created Materials, [2020] | Audience: K to Grade 3. |
Identifiers: LCCN 2018049786 (print) | LCCN 2018050705 (ebook) | ISBN 9781493868940 (eBook) | ISBN 9781493866540 (paperback)
Subjects: LCSH: Butterflies--Juvenile literature.
Classification: LCC QL544.2 (ebook) | LCC QL544.2 .R527 2020 (print) | DDC 595.78/9--dc23
LC record available at https://lccn.loc.gov/2018049786

Smithsonian

© 2019 Smithsonian Institution. The name "Smithsonian" and the Smithsonian logo are registered trademarks owned by the Smithsonian Institution.

Teacher Created Materials

5301 Oceanus Drive
Huntington Beach, CA 92649-1030
www.tcmpub.com
ISBN 978-1-4938-6654-0
© 2019 Teacher Created Materials, Inc.

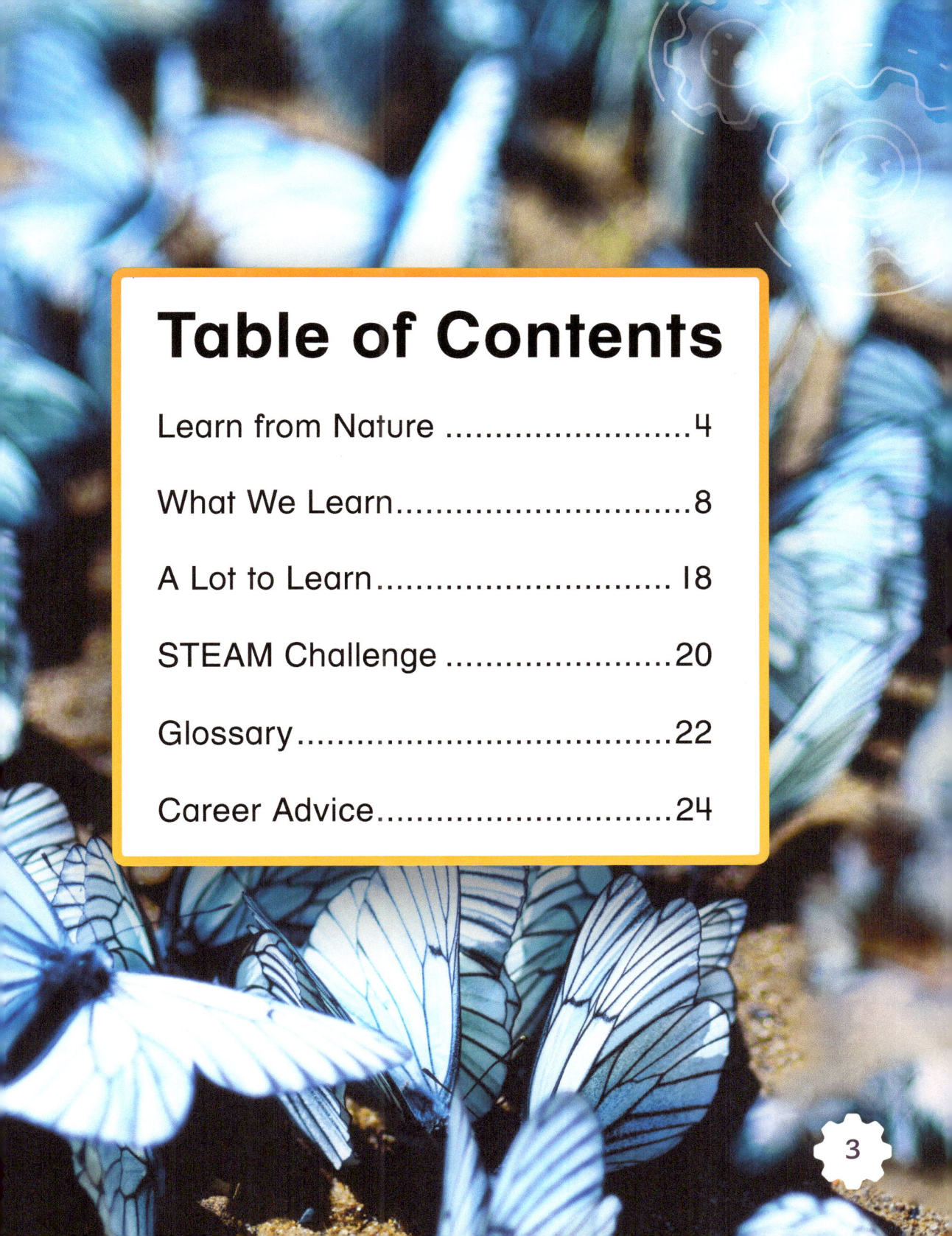

Table of Contents

Learn from Nature 4

What We Learn 8

A Lot to Learn 18

STEAM Challenge 20

Glossary 22

Career Advice 24

Learn from Nature

All living things have ways to survive in the world. We can learn from them.

A green-orb web spider spins a web.

Zebras stay together to stay safe.

Butterflies may not seem like teachers. But we can learn more from them than you might think.

A boy studies a butterfly.

The shapes on butterfly wings make the wings waterproof.

Technology & Engineering

Waterproof Wings

Butterfly wings are waterproof. Water drops do not stick to them. People learned to make **fabric** like these wings.

What We Learn

Butterflies have lots of colors and patterns. These designs help them survive. They can help us as well.

This butterfly has green and black wings.

Some butterflies have bright spots.

This butterfly has patterns of lines.

9

Colors and Patterns

Butterflies can **blend in**. This helps them hide from danger.

People can also blend in. They can hide too.

This pale cracker butterfly blends in with tree bark.

This soldier uses paint and plants to hide.

Science & Arts

Dead Leaf Butterfly

This butterfly looks like a dead leaf. It has changed to look this way. It blends in with the world around it.

Bright colors can be a warning. *Do not eat me! I may be **toxic**.*

People can use colors as warnings too.

This butterfly is toxic.

This butterfly's yellow wings warn that it may be toxic.

Parts of Wings

Butterfly wings do not stay dirty. They clean themselves.

People copied this. They made some clothes in this way.

This fabric can clean itself.

Mathematics

Window Coverings

The shapes on butterfly wings keep them clean too. Some windows are coated with patterns of the same shapes. The patterns keep windows clean.

Some butterfly wings have tiny holes. They take in a lot of sunlight.

People copied this too. Some **solar panels** are made like this.

This butterfly's wings have tiny holes in them.

This solar panel has tiny holes in it.

A Lot to Learn

There is still a lot we can learn from butterflies. What is next? Who knows? Maybe people will learn to fly!

STEAM CHALLENGE

The Problem

Many people who watch animals like to blend in with the world around them. This is called *camouflage*. Can you design a piece of fabric that an animal watcher can wear to blend in?

The Goals

- Choose a place at your school that your fabric will blend in with.
- Choose how your fabric will be used.
- Choose colors and patterns that will act as camouflage.

Research and Brainstorm
How does camouflage help keep people and animals safe? Where do people like to watch animals?

Design and Build
Design fabric to blend in with an area. Decide how a person will wear or use the fabric. What colors or patterns will you use? Create your fabric!

Test and Improve
Show your fabric to your friends. Does it blend in with the area you chose? Can you make your fabric better? Try again.

Reflect and Share
How might you be able to spot a person in camouflage? Could blending in ever be a problem for a person?

Glossary

blend in

fabric

solar panels

toxic

Career Advice
from Smithsonian

Do you want to create products based on animals? Here are some tips to get you started.

"Plant flowers that butterflies like. Then, you can study the butterflies up close!"
— *James Gagliardi, Horticulturalist*

"If you love nature and insects, then go exploring! See what you can learn from the world around you." — *Nate Erwin, Former Manager of the O. Orkin Insect Zoo and Butterfly Pavilion*

www.ingramcontent.com/pod-product-compliance
Lightning Source LLC
Chambersburg PA
CBHW041122070526
44584CB00002B/244